CONNECT WITH ELECTRICITY

HOW LEDs WORK

BY JAMES ROLAND

LERNER PUBLICATIONS ◆ MINNEAPOLIS

To my wife, Heidi, the light of my life.
—J.R.

Lerner Publications Company
A division of Lerner Publishing Group, Inc.
241 First Avenue North
Minneapolis, MN USA 55401

For reading levels and more information, look up this title at www.lernerbooks.com.

Main body text set in Aptifer Slab LT Pro 12/18.
Typeface provided by Linotype AG.

Library of Congress Cataloging-in-Publication Data

Names: Roland, James, author.
Title: How LEDs work / by James Roland.
Description: Minneapolis : Lerner Publications, [2017] | Series: Connect with electricity | Audience: Ages 8–11. | Audience: Grades 4 to 6. | Includes bibliographical references and index.
Identifiers: LCCN 2015038217| ISBN 9781512407808 (lb : alk. paper) | ISBN 9781512410099 (eb pdf)
Subjects: LCSH: Light emitting diodes—Juvenile literature. | Electric lighting—Equipment and supplies—Juvenile literature.
Classification: LCC TK7871.89.L53 R65 2017 | DDC 621.3815/22—dc23

LC record available at http://lccn.loc.gov/2015038217

Manufactured in the United States of America
1-39352-21164-2/26/2016

CONTENTS

LEDs are used with sensors in touch screens for TVs, phones, and other devices.

What if you could have a lightbulb that was as bright as any other bulb, saved you money, didn't need much energy to work, was usually cool to the touch, and lasted practically forever? Well, it already exists! It's called a light-emitting diode, or LED. LEDs are used in toys, streetlights, flashing signs, cell phones, TV remotes, computers, and much more. Maybe you're using a book light containing an LED to read this very page.

LEDs are truly changing the way we light our world. They differ from standard lightbulbs in many ways, and in the coming years, they will be used more and more to light homes, cities, and even spacecraft.

So let's check out what LEDs are made of and how they work. You'll see how they're used in items ranging from digital alarm clocks to giant screens at sports stadiums. You'll also learn why LEDs are the best options to solve some serious lighting problems as well as how they're likely to be used in the future.

CHAPTER ONE

WHAT ARE LEDs?

For a tiny invention, the LED plays a big part in how we live every day. You'll find these high-tech lights illuminating your home and the streetlights outside. They're used in light-up necklaces and in the International Space Station. And the use of LEDs is only likely to grow as scientists discover more ways to take advantage of these mini marvels.

NASA uses LEDs to help plants such as this lettuce grow on the International Space Station.

But is an LED really that different from a traditional lightbulb? For many years, the lightbulbs used in almost all lamps and light fixtures have been incandescent bulbs. That's a glass bulb surrounding a thin wire thread called a filament. When the filament is heated by an electric current, it produces light. Over time, however, that filament will burn out. That means these bulbs need to be replaced fairly often.

Another common lightbulb is a fluorescent light. You've probably seen these long

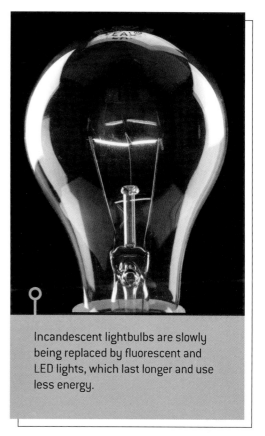

Incandescent lightbulbs are slowly being replaced by fluorescent and LED lights, which last longer and use less energy.

tubes, which light offices, stores, garages, and even closets and bathrooms. Fluorescent bulbs are filled with mercury vapor. When electrical energy runs through the vapor, it creates ultraviolet light, which can't be seen by the human eye. But the tubes are coated with a chemical compound called phosphor. When the phosphor is exposed to ultraviolet light, it emits a light we can see.

LEDs don't need heat or mercury vapor to produce light. In an LED, light emerges when electricity runs through the combination of materials that make up the LED.

SEMICONDUCTOR MATERIALS

In the world of electronics, all materials can be classified as conductors, semiconductors, or insulators. A conductor allows electricity to easily pass through it. Copper and aluminum are good conductors. An insulator blocks the flow of electricity. Rubber and plastic are common insulators. That's why you see them wrapped around electrical wires. A semiconductor is basically a solid in between an insulator and a conductor. Electricity can pass through it, but not as easily as it can through a conductor.

LEDs are a lot like computer chips. Both are made of semiconductor materials. Silicon, for example, is a semiconductor used in computer chips.

Many LEDs contain a silvery semiconductor material called gallium. To make an LED, layers of semiconductor materials are compressed into an ultrathin, tiny, square chip. The semiconductor part of an LED is about the size of a grain of pepper.

But you can't just throw together any semiconductors and hope the LED works. One layer of the chip must contain extra electrons. Changes in the semiconductor material's electrons are caused by adding other elements, such as zinc or phosphorous. This process is called doping. When combined with a semiconductor material, these other elements can add electrons or holes that the electrons will bond with to create light.

The negatively charged layer receives electrons from a terminal called a cathode. The positively charged layer gets electricity from

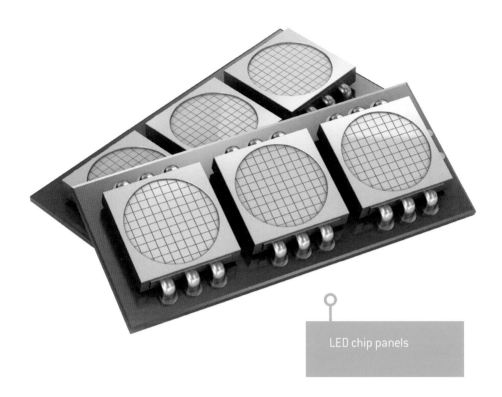

LED chip panels

a terminal called an anode. Terminals are conductors. When there are two terminals, a semiconductor device is called a diode. So every light-emitting diode has two terminals.

When an electric current runs through an LED's terminals, electrons and positively charged particles called holes move toward each other. The positive particles are called holes because they contain empty spaces that used to hold electrons.

Electricity could come from a battery or through a cord plugged into a wall outlet or a generator. Think of turning on a flashlight. The batteries inside send an electrical charge to the terminals, which then start the movement of the electrons and holes in the LED. The area where the two oppositely charged particles meet is

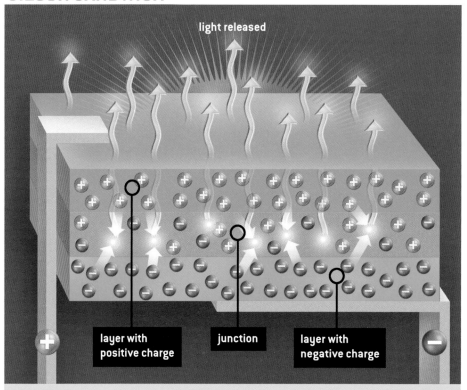

light released

layer with positive charge

junction

layer with negative charge

This diode releases a light when the electrons from the negatively charged layer at the bottom and the holes from the positively charged layer at the top connect in the middle at the junction.

called a junction. When an electron passes over the junction and connects with a hole, the connection gives off light.

All this activity happens very quickly and very often, so it appears as though the LED is shining a very steady light. But in reality, LED light is made of countless little bursts of light energy called photons.

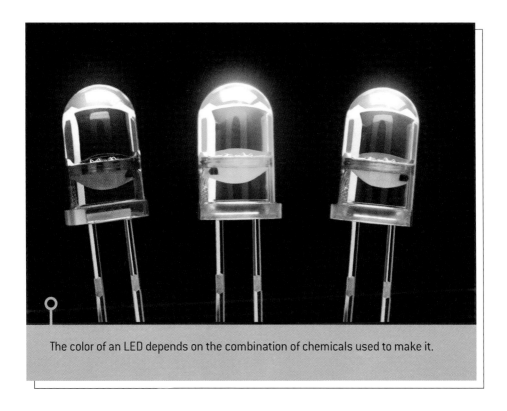

The color of an LED depends on the combination of chemicals used to make it.

HISTORY OF LEDs

Although LEDs have only recently begun to replace incandescent lights, scientists first observed this light technology more than a century ago. Two men deserve credit, even though they never met.

In 1907 British radio engineer Henry Round was experimenting with silicon carbide in radio transmissions. This material was used in early radios to collect information transmitted in radio waves. That's when he first noticed electroluminescence, which is what happens when a material gives off light as an electric current goes through it.

That same year, Russian inventor Oleg Losev also noted the light-emitting qualities of silicon carbide in radio equipment. Both men continued to experiment with this new LED technology for many years. In 1927 Losev wrote about potential uses for LEDs. He noted how the strength of the electric current that runs through a semiconductor can affect the type of light that's emitted. And he observed that, unlike Thomas Edison's lightbulbs, LEDs did not require heat to produce light.

Through the years, researchers discovered more LED colors and more uses for these little electronic gems. Other leaps in history include the 1961 discovery by two Texas Instruments (TI) engineers of an LED that produces infrared light. Infrared light has a wavelength a tiny bit greater than the red end of the color spectrum, so it's invisible to the human eye. It can be detected by the heat it radiates or with special sensors. The engineers detected that first infrared LED with the help of a special kind of microscope that can pick up images around the edge of the color spectrum.

A year later, Illinois engineer Nick Holonyak Jr. invented the first red LED of visible light while working for General Electric (GE). Since then, the red LED has been used as a light showing that a device is on. For many years, digital clocks and calculators used a display of red LEDs to display numbers and letters.

The 1970s were a big decade for different colored LEDs. In 1972 M. George Craford created the yellow LED while working at the

Engineer Nick Holonyak Jr. invented the first red LED of visible light while working for General Electric (GE) in 1962.

chemical company Monsanto. He also developed a brighter red LED. That same year, Herbert Maruska and Jacques Pankove created the first violet LED. Thomas Pearsall followed that up four years later with a high-brightness LED.

Clearly, quite a lot of research, activity, and technology are packed into that tiny device.

CHAPTER TWO

DIFFERENT TYPES OF LEDs

The next time you're at a supermarket or a hardware store, take a look at all the different types of lightbulbs for sale. You'll see fluorescent lights and incandescent bulbs of many sizes and strengths. Our society uses lighting in many different ways, for outdoor spotlights, big and small lamps, overhead room lights, fancy chandeliers, and other kinds of fixtures.

LED bulbs come in the same kind of variety. Miniature LEDs are among the most common. These are built into holiday lights, cell phones, digital clocks, and other devices where small, long-lasting lights are needed. And just like the traditional lightbulbs for your home, some LED bulbs are meant to be brighter or softer or larger or smaller than others. The LED bulb in a car headlight is different from the LED bulbs that fit into the light fixtures in your classroom.

The LED bulbs that fit in lamps and overhead lights usually have multiple little LEDs inside them, which makes them brighter and more powerful. High-powered LEDs are becoming more widely used in factories,

LED floodlights have dozens of small LEDs to provide a bright, long-lasting light.

science labs, and even as car headlights. While some high-powered LEDs are made up of several smaller LEDs, others are just larger, stronger, single LEDs.

Unlike tiny LEDs, these bigger, high-powered cousins can overheat. That's because they require more energy to operate than smaller LEDs. As that energy moves around in the device, more of that extra energy becomes heat rather than light.

Because of the overheating risk, high-powered LEDs must be used in a device designed to absorb heat safely. This device is called the heat sink. It usually looks like a metal collar with lots of grooves around the base of the bulb. The heat sink is designed to draw heat away from the semiconductor material.

HIGH-POWERED LED

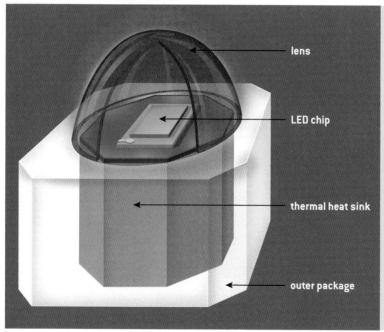

lens

LED chip

thermal heat sink

outer package

The thermal heat sink for this LED isn't visible in its outer package. Inside, it prevents the LED's semiconductor material from overheating. With the heat sink, just enough energy will power the bulb and be released out of the lens at the top.

THE COLORFUL WORLD OF LEDs

Aside from the size and strength of LEDs, one of the main things that distinguishes one from another is color. Incandescent lights can produce different-colored lights if the filament, wires, stem, and gas are covered by a colored glass bulb. But the color of an LED's light depends on its semiconductor materials. For example, gallium plus arsenide can produce a red or infrared light. Gallium nitride makes a blue LED.

Materials that combine metals and chemicals are called alloys. By changing the composition of an LED's alloy—more of one material and less of another—an engineer can change the color of its light. However, different semiconductor materials are usually needed to make different colored LEDs.

Having green and red LEDs works well for strings of holiday lights or for signs. But most of the electric lights around you are white lights. Most people prefer white light, because that is what the sun produces. White light, which is actually a combination of all the colors, is easy on the eyes.

A traditional lightbulb produces white light because white light naturally emerges when an electrical charge runs through the heated filament in the bulb.

For many years, though, people couldn't get white light from an LED. Red and green LEDs already existed, and scientists knew that the combination of red, green, and blue lights would create white LED light. So what they needed was a blue LED. The search for a blue LED kept scientists busy for decades.

LEDs in different colors are perfect for holiday decorations.

They tried all kinds of semiconductor combinations, but the blue LED eluded them.

Finally, in the 1990s, researchers discovered the right combination of materials to make a blue LED. Soon LEDs could be used for more than just the little red lights in a pocket calculator.

White LEDs can be made in two main ways. Some are made using phosphors, the same shiny chemical compound that coats the inside of fluorescent lightbulbs. Phosphors can coat a blue or ultraviolet LED and produce white light. The right mix of red, green, and blue LEDs can also generate white light. Some

NOBEL PRIZE FOR BLUE LED PIONEERS

Isamu Akasaki, a researcher, and Hiroshi Amano, a PhD student, both at Nagoya University in Japan, created the first blue LED in 1992. But its quality was poor. Around that time, at a small Japanese company called Nichia Chemicals, Japanese-born American physicist Shuji Nakamura also discovered a blue LED.

The three of them continued to develop and improve their blue LEDs throughout the 1990s and beyond. Their work helped make it possible for white LED bulbs to enter the market.

For their efforts, Akasaki, Amano, and Nakamura *(pictured, from left to right)* were given the Nobel Prize in Physics in 2014, the highest international honor given to scientists.

manufacturers use a combination of phosphors-converted LEDs and colored LEDs to create white-light products.

WAVELENGTHS AND THE HUMAN EYE

Blue LEDs are also used in devices such as Blu-ray DVD players. These use LED lasers to shine a light on a disc, which has digital information stored on it. The laser light reflects the information on the disc back to a photocell in the player, which turns into sound and images on your TV.

Blue laser wavelengths are shorter and smaller than the red wavelengths used in standard DVD players. That means the blue laser is more precise, so it can reflect back more information packed on a disc. Blu-ray discs hold more information because the blue LED

The Blu-ray disc gets its name from the blue-violet color of its laser.

laser can read more. Think about looking at a leaf with just your eyes. You'd see its color, its shape, and some details. But if you looked at the same leaf with a magnifying glass, you'd see a lot more detail. A blue LED laser is like the magnifying glass.

As light travels, it moves like an ocean wave. Picture a wave on the ocean gliding up high. That's called a crest. Then picture it dipping low. That's a trough. Light moves in a similar pattern, and we measure light by its wavelength. One wavelength is the distance between two crests or troughs. Different colors of light have different wavelengths. Blue waves are shorter than red waves, for instance.

The human eye can only see light of certain wavelengths. Wavelengths that are too short or too long are invisible to people. We can see light that travels in waves between about 400 nanometers (nm) and 750 nm. A nanometer is one billionth of a meter. Try measuring *that* with a ruler!

WAVELENGTHS AND VISIBLE SPECTRUM OF LIGHT

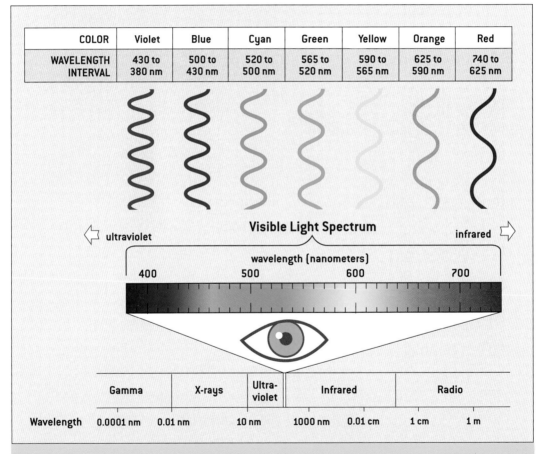

COLOR	Violet	Blue	Cyan	Green	Yellow	Orange	Red
WAVELENGTH INTERVAL	430 to 380 nm	500 to 430 nm	520 to 500 nm	565 to 520 nm	590 to 565 nm	625 to 590 nm	740 to 625 nm

Visible Light Spectrum

ultraviolet

infrared

wavelength (nanometers)

400   500   600   700

	Gamma	X-rays	Ultra-violet	Infrared	Radio
Wavelength	0.0001 nm 0.01 nm		10 nm	1000 nm 0.01 cm	1 cm 1 m

Each color of light has its own range of wavelengths. These wavelength measurements and types of light make up a spectrum.

A light's color also affects how both animals and humans behave. Baby sea turtles, for instance, are very responsive to light. They're drawn to white lights, such as moonlight, when they're born but tend to ignore amber lights. Humans, on the other hand, tend to respond positively to lights from the orange part of the spectrum. They help people relax. Lights at the blue end of the spectrum help people concentrate.

Humans cannot see ultraviolet light. It travels between 100 and 400 nm. At the other end of the spectrum, infrared light starts at about 700 nm and is also invisible. Because infrared light moves at a much longer wavelength, infrared LEDs are especially useful for devices that require light to travel long distances.

Night-vision equipment, for example, uses infrared technology. Night-vision goggles, which soldiers might wear on a secret, undercover night mission, collect and magnify all available light, including infrared light, so soldiers can see in the dark. Infrared light also gives off heat, so technology that can sense even low levels of heat can pick up infrared signals.

A special operations soldier uses night-vision goggles to see on a nighttime mission.

Infrared light is also safer than ultraviolet, or UV, light. UV light comes from the sun, but it can also be made artificially. You've probably been warned about protecting yourself from too much sun exposure. That's because UV light can damage the skin. UV light can penetrate deeper into the skin than infrared light. Artificially made UV light can also help detect counterfeit money, because it can reveal images hidden from the naked eye in large bills. The next time you see someone use a one-hundred-dollar bill to pay for groceries, the clerk may use a special LED counterfeit detector to shine the invisible light on the cash.

A light's color can tell you a lot about the light and its properties.

SOLVE IT!

GUIDING BABY SEA TURTLES

Baby sea turtles hatch in their nests on beaches near the ocean. Once they hatch, their instincts draw them toward light. But instead of crawling toward the twinkling starlight reflecting off the water, as baby sea turtles did in the past, many modern baby turtles crawl toward the bright outdoor lighting of homes and other buildings. If they don't make it to the sea, baby sea turtles often die. How could special LED lighting help guide the sea turtles in the right direction? *[The answer key is on page 35.]*

CHAPTER THREE

ADVANTAGES OF LEDs

If you've ever touched a standard lightbulb that has been on for a while, you know how hot it can get. And if you haven't, don't try it! These lights can burn you. That's because the filament must be heated to produce light. Incandescent bulbs release as much as 90 percent of their energy as heat, not light. That energy is lost and usually serves no purpose.

In contrast, almost all the energy in an LED bulb is used to produce light. LEDs waste little heat. LEDs also last much longer than incandescent bulbs because there's no filament that will eventually burn out. A quality white-LED lighting product may last for more than thirty thousand hours, compared with the average incandescent bulb's life span of about one thousand hours.

LED flashlights last longer than flashlights with incandescent bulbs and are less likely to break if dropped.

A STANDARD BULB AND AN LED

Compared with a standard incandescent lightbulb, an LED is fairly simple. Its main parts include two terminal pins to transmit an electrical current to the positive and negative sides of the diode, the diode itself, and a transparent plastic case. A traditional lightbulb has a glass or quartz outer bulb, an electrical contact point at the bottom, and two contact wires that extend up through a glass mount to a small filament or coiled thread made of a metal called tungsten. When electricity runs through the filament, the filament heats up. That lights the bulb. The incandescent bulb also includes a gas called argon to help the filament last longer.

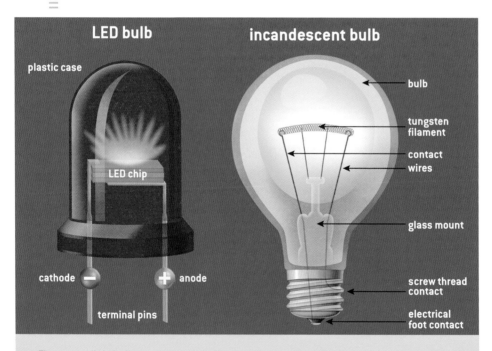

LED bulb
incandescent bulb
plastic case
LED chip
cathode — + anode
terminal pins
bulb
tungsten filament
contact wires
glass mount
screw thread contact
electrical foot contact

These two lightbulbs may seem similar, but an incandescent bulb has many more parts than an LED bulb.

One of the biggest advantages LEDs have over standard lightbulbs is their energy efficiency. But what does energy efficiency mean? It means using less power to produce the same results or getting better results with the same amount of energy.

A car that can drive farther than another car on the same amount of gas is more energy efficient. When it comes to lighting your home, an LED requires less energy than an incandescent bulb to produce the same light. That means lower energy use and costs. A way to think about energy efficiency is in watts, a unit of measure to describe power. A certain number of watts go into an LED or other type of lightbulb, but less power or fewer watts come out. In incandescent lightbulbs, some of the watts are used to create light and the rest are wasted in unused heat. In LEDs, less energy, or fewer watts, is wasted in heat.

Cities all over the world use LEDs in highway signs and streetlamps. LEDs are more expensive to build than traditional lights, but they last three to four times as long. Over time, LEDs allow cities to save millions on electricity bills.

Another big advantage of LEDs is their small size. That allows them to fit neatly into electronic circuits. LEDs can also have a very focused light stream. Incandescent lightbulbs send light out in every direction. That can be helpful in lighting a room, but for a flashlight or a reading lamp, the directed light of an LED can't be beat.

BETTER THAN FLUORESCENT BULBS

LEDs have benefits over fluorescent lightbulbs too. Fluorescent bulbs contain mercury, a metal that can make people and animals sick if it's in the air they breathe or the water they drink. Fluorescent lightbulbs that aren't properly recycled can release mercury into the environment. LEDs are more environmentally friendly than fluorescent bulbs, partly because LEDs contain no mercury.

LEDs can also be faster to use than fluorescent lights. Once an electric current runs through an LED, the light comes on. Fluorescent lights take a while to warm up. After you turn them on, they don't reach full brightness for a minute or two. If you're in a hurry, then fluorescent lights may keep you waiting a little longer. Turning fluorescent lights on and off a lot can shorten their lives. LED lights don't have that problem.

SOLVE IT!

A LIGHTED WALKWAY

You and your sister want to create a festive lighted walkway on the sidewalk outside your home. Your sister suggests using small candles in bags, but your parents say that would be a fire hazard. You've read about solar LED kits that would let you use sunlight to charge the bulbs. How might you use LEDs to create the walkway more safely? How do you think the solar kind might work? *(The answer key is on page 35.)*

CHAPTER FOUR

THE FUTURE OF LEDs

Pretend you're an astronaut on a deep-space mission. You'll spend years on your voyage. Of course you'll bring some food along, but it won't last your whole trip. Eventually, you're going to get hungry. For missions that will last years, astronauts will need to grow their own food. As you know, plants need light to grow, whether that light comes from the sun or from indoor grow lights. Could it be LEDs to the rescue?

NASA is experimenting with LEDs to find the best lighting system for those deep-space gardens. Early research suggests that red and blue LEDs can help produce nutritious plants in small spaces. NASA scientists compared red-leaf lettuce and radishes grown under light from red, green, and blue LEDs to those same plants grown under fluorescent lights. The plants grown under the LEDs had more antioxidants. Antioxidants help people stay healthy and happy. Consuming antioxidants may also help protect astronauts from radiation in space.

NASA scientists are also studying how LED lighting systems affect an astronaut's sleeping patterns. If you're exposed to too much light, even when you're tired, it can harm your ability to doze off or stay asleep. Studies show

An Italian astronaut in her sleeping bag on board the International Space Station. Astronauts use LEDs throughout the station, but blue LEDs are limited. Studies show that people exposed to blue LEDs can have trouble sleeping.

that exposure to blue LEDs reduces the amount of melatonin in a person's body. Melatonin is a hormone the body produces to help you manage your body's clock and get a good night's sleep.

Since scientists know that blue LEDs may make it harder for astronauts to get enough sleep, they can explore other colored LEDs to use in vessels on deep-space missions.

VISIBLE LIGHT COMMUNICATION

Here on Earth, LEDs also have a big future, in your home and beyond. A TV remote, for instance, has an infrared LED that sends signals to the TV to control the volume, change channels, and turn the TV on and off. An infrared light receiver in the TV changes the infrared signals into electric signals that are sent to the microprocessor in the television. The microprocessor is the part of a computer that controls everything the computer does. So when you press the volume button on your TV remote, the invisible infrared signal gets interpreted by the microprocessor as a command to make the TV louder or quieter.

Tiny changes in the pattern of the infrared signals from the remote let the TV know that you want the volume, not the channel, changed. Different buttons on the remote use different patterns of infrared light signals so the right controls on the TV are operated.

Much more is in store for LED-based communications, also known as visible light communications. Some modern communications use cell phone signals that travel to and from satellites or TV signals that are broadcast through the air. Scientists say the next big change in communications could be done with beams of LED light.

The goal is to create a network in which LEDs can communicate with one another using visible light signals. So your alarm clock might tell the lights in your room to turn on or off. The LEDs in your family's

Check out the end of your TV remote. There is probably an LED there that sends an infrared signal to the television.

car headlights might be able to communicate with the lights in other vehicles. Those LEDs could tell the driver if it's safe to change lanes or if traffic will be heavier up ahead.

Researchers are also working on a contact lens that includes a micro-LED linked to a computer. The wearer could see a computer screen only through the contact lenses—no physical computer necessary! LED-enhanced contact lenses could also help people with poor vision see better or even turn spoken words into written words displayed for people who are hearing impaired. Video game makers are interested in how an LED in a contact lens could be incorporated into gaming to make the images seem more three-dimensional or replace bulky virtual reality goggles. The LEDs would be powered by a tiny antenna that would take radio signals and turn them into electrical energy.

Companies such as Google are researching how LEDs could be used in contact lenses. One idea is to help people with diabetes test their blood sugar through tears. An LED display could give these people an early warning of changes in their blood sugar.

NIGHTLIGHTS AND CURVED SCREENS

Many uses for LEDs may seem futuristic but are already in place. For instance, LEDs can be built into wallpaper. Imagine having dozens of little LED lights all over your wall shining like stars at night. The LEDs are powered through a thin circuit board on the back of the wallpaper. The circuit board that controls the lights can be put near an electrical outlet in the wall, so power is never a problem. LED wallpaper is just for decoration, but perhaps dozens of tiny LEDs will soon take the place of a nightlight.

Samsung has created a TV screen that uses LEDs to flex from flat to curved on demand.

Another cool innovation is an organic light-emitting diode, or OLED. OLEDs are like other LEDs, except that they include organic material. You may think *organic* refers to food grown without artificial chemicals. But in chemistry, an organic material is just one that includes carbon.

LEDs made with organic materials have been used in the giant screens at sports stadiums for years. But they're also making their way into new flat screen TVs that can actually bend! Curved TV screens make you feel more like you're in the middle of the action, and the picture is often clearer than it is on a standard flat screen.

One company is working on an OLED flat screen so thin and flexible that you can peel it off one wall and place it on a magnetic mount on the wall in another room. Is there too much noise in the family room when you're watching your favorite movie? Just peel off the TV and move the screen to a quieter spot!

So you see LEDs are much more than ordinary lightbulbs. They're changing the way we light our world and outer space. They're in devices we use every day and in devices yet to be built. In fact, the next great LED innovation might come from your imagination. After all, there's a very bright future in LEDs.

BATTLE OF THE BULBS

See for yourself how much more efficient LED lightbulbs are compared with incandescent bulbs. In this science project, you'll measure the brightness of different lightbulbs and note how much power was needed to produce that light. Most of these supplies should be available through a hardware store or online, if your school doesn't have them available.

WHAT YOU'LL NEED

- pen and paper
- a small lamp
- a standard 60-watt incandescent lightbulb
- a luxmeter, or light meter, a device that measures how bright something is to the human eye
- a variety of LED lightbulbs that can fit in the lamp, such as a 1.5W bulb, a 4.5W bulb, a 6.0W bulb, or a 10.5W bulb

WHAT YOU'LL DO

1. Make a two-column table to record your findings. The first column will list the wattage of each bulb you measure. The second column will list the luxmeter measurement of each bulb.
2. Put the 60W incandescent bulb in the lamp and turn it on.
3. Place the luxmeter 3 feet (0.9 meters) from the bulb in the lamp and measure its brightness.
4. Take out the incandescent bulb and replace it with one of the LED bulbs.
5. Measure the brightness of that LED and note the bulb's wattage and its brightness in your chart.
6. Remove that LED bulb and try another. Note your findings in your chart.
7. Continue checking the brightness of each bulb and recording what you learn.

FOLLOW-UP

Which LED bulb is as bright as the incandescent bulb?
What's the difference in wattage between the incandescent bulb and the equally bright LED?

GUIDING BABY SEA TURTLES (PAGE 22)

Red and amber LEDs shine on a wavelength that isn't as bright as older, incandescent lightbulbs. By replacing old outdoor lights with LEDs that function at a lower level of visible light, you can save more baby sea turtles. Florida lawmakers have recently created laws requiring dimmer lights, and the number of baby sea turtles dying on their way toward civilization is dropping.

A LIGHTED WALKWAY (PAGE 27)

A solar-powered LED system would allow a battery to charge during the day and then provide enough energy to power colorful LED lights placed along the walkway. You could fit each little solar panel, battery, and LED in a clear jar and line up several jars on the sides of the path so they don't present a walking hazard. As you've learned, little LEDs don't get hot, so these lanterns won't be a fire hazard, and there won't be a risk of anything melting. And because LEDs can last for thousands of hours, your walkway lights should last for a long time too.

─────────────────────────────────────○

anode: the positively charged terminal in an LED

cathode: the negatively charged terminal in an LED

circuit: a path of at least two points that carries an electric current

diode: a semiconductor device with two terminals, the cathode and anode, that usually allow an electric current to flow in only one direction

electron: the part of an atom with a negative electrical charge

fluorescent lightbulb: an electric lamp that's coated on the inside with a material that contains mercury. Electrons from the cathode hit the material with ultraviolet light, which then produces visible white light.

gallium: the main element in the semiconductors used to make LEDs

incandescent lightbulb: an electric light source that emits light when the filament inside the glass covering is heated

light-emitting diode (LED): a semiconductor device that produces light when an electric current runs through it

semiconductor: a solid material that transmits electricity under certain conditions. A semiconductor is usually one solid chemical element or a compound of elements.

SELECTED BIBLIOGRAPHY ──────────────────○

"Blue LEDs—Filling the World with New Light." Royal Swedish Academy of Sciences. Accessed September 8, 2015. http://www.nobelprize.org/nobel_prizes/physics /laureates/2014/popular-physicsprize2014.pdf.

"LED Basics." Office of Energy Efficiency & Renewable Energy. Accessed September 8, 2015. http://energy.gov/eere/ssl/led-basics.

"LEDs and OLEDs." Edison Tech Center. Accessed September 6, 2015. http://www .edisontechcenter.org/LED.html.

"Top 8 Things You Didn't Know about LEDs." US Department of Energy, June 4, 2013. http://energy.gov/articles/top-8-things-you-didn-t-know-about-leds.

Cook, Trevor. *Awesome Experiments for Curious Kids.* London: Arcturus, 2012.
Check out this book full of experiments with light, heat, electricity, magnetism, and more!

Diodes and LEDs
http://www.explainthatstuff.com/diodes.html
You can learn a lot about electricity and different types of diodes at this site.

Easy LED Circuit Project
http://sciencewithkids.com/Experiments/Energy-Electricity-Experiments/easy-LED
-circuit-project.html
Try these instructions to build your own LED circuit.

Energy.gov: Lighting
http://www.energy.gov/public-services/homes/saving-electricity/lighting
Visit this site to learn more about what the US government is doing to promote energy-efficient lighting.

Marsico, Katie. *Key Discoveries in Physical Science.* Minneapolis: Lerner Publications, 2015. Get to know the scientists and engineers who figured out the rules and theories behind electricity, and see how they set the stage for modern LED experiments.

Monroe, Ronald. *What Is Electricity?* New York: Crabtree, 2012.
Explore these real-life examples that will help you understand how electricity is created, stored, and moved.

Science with Kids
http://sciencewithkids.com/science-facts/facts-about-LEDs.html
Check out this site to learn more about how LEDs are made and how they work.

Walker, Sally M. *Investigating Electricity.* Minneapolis: Lerner Publications, 2012.
Discover some unusual properties of electricity with these safe, fun experiments.

INDEX

PHOTO ACKNOWLEDGMENTS

The images in this book are used with the permission of: © iStockphoto .com/da-vooda (electronic icon); © iStockphoto.com/Kubkoo (color dots background); © iStockphoto.com/alenaZ0509 (zigzag background); © iStockphoto.com/Sashatigar (robots and electrical microschemes); © Robert Daly/CaiaimageGetty Images, p. 4; NASA/Frankie Martin, p. 6; © Todd Strand/Independent Picture Service, p. 7; © Alexandr Mitiuc/ Dreamstime.com, p. 9; Rob Schuster, pp. 10, 15, 20, 24; © Steven Puetzer/ Photodisc/Getty Images, p. 11; AP Photo/The News-Gazette, Tom Roberts, p. 13; © iStockphoto.com/CamiloTorres, p. 14; © Cliff/flickr.com (CC BY 2.0), p. 17; Kyodo/Newscom, p. 18; © imageBROKER/SuperStock, p. 19; © Stocktrek Images/SuperStock, p. 21; © iStockphoto.com/Aneese, p. 22; © iStockphoto.com/Chris Bernard Photography Inc., p. 23; © iStockphoto .com/shaunl, p. 25; Johnson Space Center/NASA, p. 29; © MAHATHIR MOHD YASIN/Shutterstock.com, p. 30; AP Photo/Google/REX, p. 31; © Hel080808/ Dreamstime.com, p. 32.

Cover: © iStockphoto.com/adventtr (television); © iStockphoto.com/ da-vooda (electronic icon); © iStockphoto.com/Kubkoo (color dots background); © iStockphoto.com/alenaZ0509 (zigzag background); © iStockphoto.com/Sashatigar (robots and electrical microschemes).